D1594983

Become Your Masterpiece

Become Your Masterpiece

A Poetic Symphony of Wisdom, Guidance, Tools and Techniques for Transforming Your Life

Carlton J. Buller

First Edition
Published by FairWeather Publications in North Miami Beach, Florida

Cover design by: Ese Gift Osakwe
Interior conceptualized, designed and created by Carlton J Buller
Edited by Carlton J. Buller

Library of Congress Control Number: 2023904566

Buller, Carlton J.
Become Your Masterpiece/Carlton J. Buller

ISBN: 978-0-9701238-3-1

Every reasonable attempt has been made to identify owners of copyright.
Errors or omissions will be corrected in subsequent editions.

Publisher's Cataloging-in-Publication data

Names: Buller, Carlton J., author.
Title: Become your masterpiece: a poetic symphony of wisdom and guidance / Carlton J. Buller.
Description: Includes bibliographical references. | North Miami Beach, FL: FairWeather Publications, 2023.
Identifiers: LCCN: 2023904566 | ISBN: 978-0-9701238-3-1
Subjects: LCSH Self-actualization (Psychology). | Success. | Poetry, American. | Self-help. | BISAC Body, Mind & Spirit / Inspirational & Personal Growth
Classification: LCC BF637.S8 .B85 2023 | DDC 158.1--dc23

Dedication

This book is dedicated to all survivors of childhood maltreatment.
May you soon find a way to become all that you were meant to be.

Contents

Acknowledgments

Without the support of my family this book would not have been possible. I am extremely grateful for all that they continue to do.

I would also like to thank my dear friend, Sam Phoenix Jones, for her invaluable insights, which certainly contributed to making this book what it is.

My love affair with poetry began in high school when, as a junior, I was for the first time treated to a display of soaring oratory by Don Hernan Ochaeta, my English teacher at the time. I will forever be grateful to him for influencing me in this direction just by being whom he naturally was.

As well, I am thankful for all others who have impacted my life in one way or another. The lessons you taught me, knowingly or not, have all brought me to this point.

I honor you all through this work of art and the positive impact it will hopefully have on the lives of those who come in contact with it.

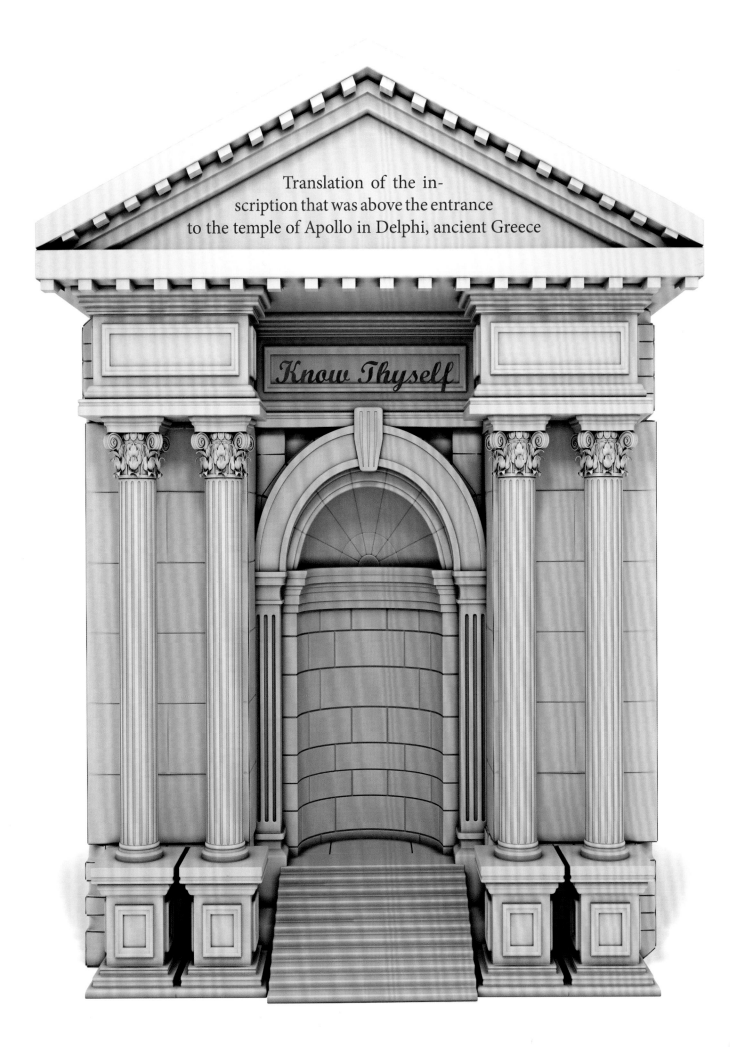

Translation of the in-
scription that was above the entrance
to the temple of Apollo in Delphi, ancient Greece

Know Thyself

Introduction

Between these covers you will find an eclectic collection of poems that are best categorized as transformational poetry. Arranged in a very specific pattern designed to take you on a journey that is at once informational and inspirational, they are intended as a gift to those seekers who want to improve their lives and are ready for some thought provoking information about how exactly to do that.

Of course, if you can be entertained, inspired and informed all at the same time that would be the best of all possible outcomes. The goal of this material is to do exactly that.

This book is designed and presented as a coffee table book. It is not intended to be stuffed away on the top shelf of some book case after you have read it. Front and center is an ideal location where it can serve as a conversation piece for family, friends and guests. You may also want to keep it within easy reach for those moments when you repeatedly succumb to the urge to revisit that one piece that touched you in a special way and demands rereading to get to an even deeper understanding of the many layers of discovery it evokes.

As you progress through the various pages try to meld your consciousness with the mind of the author. Take note of the light humor that is sparingly interspersed. Feel the lightheartedness he experienced on his creative journey even as he tackled some of the most important topics we tend to avoid. And enjoy the story telling aspect of this type of transformational poetry.

Finally, if you feel so inclined, please don't hesitate to pass it on to someone you believe can benefit from its message. Know that this author never takes credit for anything he writes. It feels like my hand is guided every single time I do.

It is my sincere hope that all who come in contact with the message contained within these pages will be imbued with renewed hope and see it as the impetus you need to begin the transformation journey that will move you closer to ultimately realizing your full potential.

Stillness

Fear not that I blunder
When seemingly alone I ponder
Worry not for me
If a recluse I appear to be

And if congested roads I do not travel
It is not that my life is soon to unravel
Or even that I am somber and morose
Instead, enthralled by whispers of wondrous prose

And music and song in silent verse
I marvel at the absolute brilliance of the universe
In concealing the wisdom of the ages
Deep within the serene pages

Of nothingness

And stillness

Twilight

Crystal clear blue
Gradually fades to gray
Bidding adieu
Waves cease to break and spray

Precocious pigeons retire to shadowy eaves
No safer place is there to stay
Once rhythmically fluttering leaves
Now only gently sway

On land and darkening sea
Daylight slowly surrenders its display
Reminiscent of a Christmas tree
Twinkling lights seemingly now come out to play

As orange hues
Grow dim and melt away
And nightingales soulfully sing the blues
To mourn the passing day

Moonshine

We sat and watched my siblings and me
Way back when we had no TV
The town was small
Four floors were considered tall

But instead of frightening
The thick dark blanket was so inviting
As night enveloped day
And twinkling lights began a visual essay

About a trillion chickens covering the earth
Carefully watched over as they pecked at dirt
By an ever vigilant, patient mother hen
Who even way back then

Seemingly our actions misconstrued
Concluding we were part of her brood
Laying out a magic carpet
To protect us from getting wet

As we traversed the golden highway
That shimmered all the way to the end of the bay
Lighting the way
Almost as bright as day

So we could easily and safely follow
The reflection of her halo
As she silently beckoned for all to see
All the while entertaining my siblings and me

A running start, a quick take off
Gradual ascension to freedom aloft
Soaring effortlessly on featherless wings
Relishing all the happiness it brings

Flight

Feels perfectly natural this ability to fly
Becoming almost one with the sky
Idly soaring over meadows and moors
Even as darkness obscures

Never ever sufficient to prevent
Absence of light actually triggers the event
When I lay down is when I rise
Having barely had time to close my **eyes**

I take my place in the friendly skies
Totally free from all earthly ties
So very real it seems to me
This flight of fantasy in my dream I see

Ever see a movie where a woman dreams of visiting some faraway island where she picks up a shell on a beach and then wakes up with the same shell clasped firmly in her hand?

"Dream" is the real-life equivalent of that!

Easy to see:
How a person could fall asleep and dream of someone in a faraway place ... happens all the time this kind of dream

Easy to understand:
How a person could fall asleep and dream of someone in a faraway place falling over a cliff ... after all it's just a dream, right?

Not so easy to imagine:
A person falling asleep and dreaming of someone in a distant city falling over a cliff and finding out the next day that it actually happened ... what?

Difficult to believe:
That a person could fall asleep and dream of someone in a distant city falling over a cliff at the same time that it actually happened ... whoa ... hold on a minute.

Hard to accept:
That the person having that dream didn't just have a dream but was traveling out of his body and actually saw it happen ... but he was there

Impossible to prove:
How would a person traveling out of his body and interacting in an event taking place somewhere else be able to prove that he was actually there? ... good question!

No one would ever think:
That a person could fall asleep and dream of someone falling off a cliff and then read about it the next day in the paper word for word exactly the way he dreamt it ...
Yeah, maybe

Dream

Even if they did:
They could not accept that the dreamer confirmed that the dream happened at the same time as the actual event because he went to bed just before the time the paper said that it happened and got up to use the bathroom an hour later when the paper said the rescue was completed ... sounds about right

So how then could they possibly believe:
That a person actually fell asleep, traveled out of his body, witnessed a man fall off a cliff, watched the rescue operation, interacted with some entities in the dream and brought back something that would actually prove he was there? ... Are you crazy?

Neither am I:
But the whole purpose of the event was never about convincing anyone other than the dreamer himself that he is fully capable of this and so much more and he just needs to allow himself to accept what he already knows ... he did, sort of

If you were the dreamer would you?
See, the dreamer was torn because he accepted the reality of the event but viewed the evidence he brought back as simply the discrepancy that it apparently was and left it at that ... what would you have done?

So, what was this discrepancy?
Imagine going to visit a hospital in a different city and seeing a sign at the entrance with the name that everyone recognizes including you ... That's the discrepancy?

Hold your horses:
So anyway, the following day you see a story in your local newspaper about a hospital in the same city you visited but you don't know it is the same hospital because they use a different name ... So?

There's so much about life that we don't understand.

Now, imagine this happening to the dreamer:

In his dream the name of the hospital where the rescued man is taken is San Francisco General, But the newspaper story said they took him to Mission Emergency ... Ok

Stick with me now:

So the dreamer decided he just had a really weird dream but it must not have been an extraordinary dream because he didn't even get the name of the hospital right ... Uh huh

Here's the clincher:

Over the course of the next year the dreamer is increasingly troubled and eventually investigates further only to be told by the newspaper archivist that the two places are one and the same. Because the emergency entrance of San Francisco General is located on Mission Street that's the name commonly used by the locals ... Wow!

Now do you understand?

The one apparent discrepancy is no discrepancy at all but is actually the proof he needed to convince himself that he could not simply be recalling the newspaper story because they had used a different name which wasn't even known to him ... Yeah, me too

So, now do you acknowledge?

That a person can travel out of his body in a dream, visit a faraway place and witness an event taking place as it is happening in real time, and bring back proof that it actually happened? ...

Hmm, let me get back to you on that!

We've barely begun to scratch the surface with respect to gaining knowledge of our true capabilities.

Be generous with your time.
Be generous with your love.
Be generous with your knowledge.
And yes, of course, be kind.

Blessings

I awoke today and tallied the score
Opened my eyes and added one more
And then another when I got out of bed
And had some eggs with a slice of bread

As the count increased each hour of the day
It dawned on me I had to give some away
So I started subtracting as I blessed each thing
But it further increased instead of decreasing

I later learned through principled living
The very act of giving
Multiplies each blessing
And I finally understood what I'd been missing

It is equally important to give and receive
But in giving to receive only yourself you deceive
Receiving fulfills a far nobler purpose
Allowing others the opportunity to be generous

Generosity is not just about money.

What's the most important room in your home?

14

Morning Show

There was a time when accompanied by his thoughts alone he would go
And position himself appropriately for the morning show
Then silently allow the pearls to come and go with little regard for the power they possessed
But soon suspecting intrinsic value he hadn't previously assessed

He began prematurely to rush back out the door
Trying to capture them before they were no more
Eventually, recognizing the futility
Of this activity

He resolved to arm himself with paper and pen
Before proceeding to enter the den
But he's acquired a new best friend
Which accompanies him even to earth's end

And now sitting on top of his lap is his laptop
Even as he perches atop
The most appropriate vantage point for observing
And even for capturing

If I may
The comings and goings of the wisdom of the day

Make the most of those precious moments!

Teach

Grow

Learn

Transform

Transcend

Transform

I often wonder
About life and death
Both before and after
We draw our last breath

Is the journey similar in any way
To coming to this sphere?
Do we begin a new solar day
With hopefulness or fear?

After we have expired
Do we ever forget
Knowledge acquired
While casting a silhouette?

Cycle of Life

When a person is dying
Is he ever aware
Where he is flying
After finally leaving here?

Are we galactic travelers
Teaching and learning
As life continually recurs
According to each yearning?

Or is this our last chance
To literally transcend the hearse
And finally dance
Through the ever expanding universe?

BORN TO
LEARN

BORN TO TEACH

LEARN TO TEACH

TEACH TO LEARN

If we're born into a family according to lessons needed
Some to be taught, others heeded
What does mine say about giving and receiving, love and forgiveness
Understanding and kindness

And the extent to which my trust
Is robust?
How about compassion, patience and humility
Even empathizing ability?

Are there points to earn
For painful lessons we learn?
What about respect and gratitude, laughing and crying
Even getting old and dying?

And how will I know
When I've learned enough, or that others can grow
From what I was fortunate to teach?
Will that be when a state of spiritual enlightenment I finally reach?

If I finish early must I leave right away?
So if I'm old and gray I hadn't finished teaching or learning and I got to stay?

And when finally I kick the bucket
Will it be because with all my heart I've learned and I've taught and there is no longer anything in it?

Lessons

I'm conceived
I'm born
I sit up
I try to stand
But for a while all I do is creep

I ask
Tell
Hear
Feel
And sometimes too I even weep

I smell
I taste
I eat
I drink
And even find the time to sleep

I study
I Work
I Dream
And play
And oftentimes I ponder deep

I talk
I walk
And run
And ride
And also get to drive a jeep

I camp
And Swim
And Fish
And Hike
And then I climb a hill so steep

And looking down from atop that hill
Wondering if I ever will
Understanding I may never still
Find a purpose I can forever fulfill

I continue trudging as I often do
Through hills and valleys
And streets and alleys
Thinking I am long overdue

And if it cannot find me
Perhaps I will find it
Yet still 'The Truth' I cannot see
So I continue to sit

And stand, and run, and ride, and walk,
And study, and work, and sleep, and pray,
And taste, and smell, and ask, and tell, and talk,
And live…, and breathe…, and dream…, and play

On this never ending merry-go-round
Until finally one day full circle come it may
And suddenly realizing me it has found
What in the world on that day will I say?

divine intervention

There
are moments
in time when spirit
intervenes in our lives

Divine Intervention

I walked alone; my head was bowed
Heard my name being called out loud
Looked around no one was there
All alone in the middle of nowhere

The second time I heard the voice
Tried to ignore it; had no choice
For still no one was there
Then I realized there was nothing to fear

For that voice in reality
Was in and out and all around me
And I had simultaneously sensed and heard
Become aware, perhaps inferred

This mass of energy
Reminiscent of telenergy
Creating sound of particular wavelength
With sufficient strength

For me to perceive or hear
Somewhere without or within each ear
In some place capable of receiving
Or even preconceiving

And while I never knew
Who
Or what was trying to contact me
I eventually concluded it might very well be

That the only reason I was being contacted
Was to make me aware that such a force existed
So that I might properly conceive and believe
The reality of future messages I was to receive

There are no coincidences. Everything is connected.

Spiritual Nourishment

Way up high and far away
Exactly where I cannot say
A silent stream braves cranny and nook
Eventually, becoming a brook

Before long, a waterfall
Down the mountain does fall
Frothing noisily to the valley floor
This brook, then suddenly brook no more

Soon begins a gradual flow
Not too fast and not too slow
All the while nourishing
And flourishing

As it meanders through the vastness
Of your unsuspecting consciousness

The worst things that
happen to us are often the
best things that happen to us.

Meaning and Purpose

If I my steps could go back and retrace
Mindful of opportunities missed along the way
I could not just my missteps seek to replace
With perfect execution of everything I do and say

My life could be filled with affluence and success
And all the trappings of the rich and famous
From fancy cars I could possess
To mansions truly incredulous

My purpose though would be ill served
And perhaps my existence not nearly so fulfilling
For if one really wants what is deserved
A few challenges in life can be so revealing

Better instead to find meaning and purpose
In whatever circumstances eventually befall us

How do you know?

Sense it before you commence it!

Choices

I think about the life I might have had
Had I made choices that weren't half bad
Perhaps a wife and children of my own
Possibly by now all grown

And all the accoutrements of success
Including material things I could possess
But I might not have been the same lad
Maybe not even had the same choices I had

Had I ignored alternatives presented
And chosen the path more frequented
For different choices surely
Would have been made purely

In the context of the particular set
Of circumstances. And it's almost a sure bet
That different choices
Would also have altered those circumstances

And I might have found
That I had to navigate around
A whole new set of challenges
Designed to bring about the changes

Necessary to fulfill
The purpose of my existence and will
Of the universe
Which through this lifetime I currently traverse

Contemplation

The Precursor to "Informed Action"

Enlightenment

1
Trudging along a bumpy road
Burdened by a heavy load
Wondering how much longer
Before I'd buckle under

2
I stopped to sit
And rest a bit
And surrendered to the temptation
To engage in contemplation

3
For I could see
In the field next to me
Seeds a farmer had sown
Now full size had grown

4
And him now busy harvesting
The just reward of his planting
And presently it dawned on me
That, had he

5
No faith his seed would ever grow
His seed he would never sow
So up I got
And began to trot

6
In a better mood
My faith renewed
My burden lightened
My mind … forever enlightened

2
Energy in form
That's easy to recognize
Accepted as the norm
Reality it most certainly belies

1
Audible vibrations
Registering on tympanums
Sound orchestrations
Recognized by cerebrums

3
For just as surely
Though not widely accepted
Information clearly
Has other means of being transmitted

Knowledge

6
Neither arbitrary action
Nor the result of conscious thought
Simply a conditioned reaction
To knowledge spiritually brought

4
A boding
A sense
Of foreboding
Even becoming tense

5
Or the hint of a smile
Perhaps in the eyes as well
Lasting for a while
Coursing through each cell

Grist

A farmer heads home with his mule and cart
Loaded with produce and a big round stump
The mule is old and thin as a dart
The stump smooth except for a bump

The artist sitting by the road
Perhaps his masterpiece this could be
Now alert he positively glowed
A piece of art all he could see

Dreaming of making his stump into a stool
The farmer tired after a very long day
Gently coaxes along the mule
Whose only thought some nice dry hay

Suddenly approaching driving like a fool
A bright red flash like a speeding bullet
Startling everyone, especially the mule
Who suddenly flees like a frightened pullet

Off the cart the stump goes flying
Even the bump couldn't keep it from rolling
Split in two in the road it's now lying
Shaking his fist the farmer glowering

In the distance a vanishing dream
For both the farmer and the artist
No masterpieces it would seem
But for the poet certainly grist

Awakening begins when we least expect it. And we are hardly aware or able to recognize what is happening.

Glimpses

Silently it billows
Like soft, feathery pillows
Punctuating the clear, blue skies
While surreptitiously it belies

1

The turbulent interior
Of the serene exterior
Of this always shifting
Forever drifting

2

Eventually
And temporarily
Dissipate, and a moment of calm
Does permeate the invisible, quiet storm

4

Not so wise old
Searching soul
And like the clouds
So too internal shrouds

3

41

Inspiration initially comes
via fleeting moments.

We often have but a few seconds to
capture them before they are no more.

Guidance

Mysteriously again it materialized
More like an awareness inside, deep down
As always, unable to be categorized
This time vivid, more shape than sound

Other times occasionally whispering
Wisdom and guidance 'twas there to deliver
Then less feeling more like hearing
A crystal clear meandering river

Rambling round the solar plexus
Not much lower, sometimes higher
Always between the gut and hypothalamus
Disappearing again into thin ether

Streaming

When the seeker seeks and gets an answer he is trying to find
It doesn't just come from somewhere deep inside his mind
Instead, having opened a portal to some profound thing either in or on the outside
He or she has communicated with a force that cannot be denied

When an answer mysteriously comes to someone who is seeking such
It may not be that the seeker finds what she is looking for so much
As it is the case that the information may actually have been seeking her
Anticipated by that force unseen and delivered in a way that she would prefer

When seeker and unseen force in this type of interaction collaborate
The unseen force provides exactly what is requested and does not elaborate
Teachers not mind readers such entities are
Better the seeker should take responsibility by far

Unseen forces offer us a lot
Unlimited resources are what they've got
Treasure troves of information ready to be retrieved
Available only to those who are ready for what is to be received

Yet, ignored by all conventional wisdom these very same forces
Willingly catering to the every whim of their sources
Their basic needs not nearly as extravagant as ours
So often unrequited by mere mortals equipped solely with earthly powers

Have only ever needed and wanted to serve
Moreover, their kind and selfless acts deserve
No less than what would cost us nothing, and besides
These are the precise means by which each unseen force provides

Would in fact be the very thing that satisfies
And in the end their existence justifies
For as much as we need them they need us even more
And so we need to seek their insight more ... and more ... and more

Doesn't mean it can't happen. So, if you encounter him don't automatically send him away. He may have an important message for you.

Wisdom

When the Universe prepares to impart a lesson to some random soul
It doesn't just send to the person's door a wise old man with a pole
Instead, the teacher in the most inconspicuous manner then arrives
For it is not self-aggrandizement on which he or she thrives

When the teacher conveys a lesson to the student
It is through a method deemed most effective and prudent
And typically it is by example
And the student will likely not know he or she is getting a sample
Of the benevolence of the Universe in action
Without regard for short term satisfaction

When a student in this fashion receives a lesson from the teacher
Never the same as listening to a preacher
Immediately not knowing he or she is being taught
At some other point in time becoming distraught
Finally desperate for any solution
He or she arrives at the incredible realization

In the vast expanse of time and space
It is wise to remember that all things have their time and place
And with all its infinite wisdom
The Universe always creates the right outcome

Be still and know.

Oftentimes, like two way mirrors
They act as a porthole
For viewing what occurs
Deep within your soul

Other times, they're not so clear
Whether dry
Or shedding a tear
From emotions gone awry

Through open eyes you look
Closing them when you want to see
Or hear the sound of a babbling brook
Running wild and free

For that is when the third one opens
Unlocking perceptive ability
Much the same as a telephoto lens
Enhancing clairvoyant acuity

The Present

It's been said that today is a gift — the present
But it doesn't last
Is never re-sent
And leaves you holding onto the past

Yearning for something greater to be
Hoping it will set you free
You close your eyes
And fantasize
To see what you can see

You sense you're here for a special purpose
Not to be glamorous
Neither bourgeoisie
Yourself you try to hypnotize
To discern what it might be

Numerous possibilities immediately appear
Several vivid, others unclear
All attractive you must agree
You try your best to recognize
Which one holds the key

Suddenly, you receive the greatest insight
Simply focus on what feels right
Whether just one or a potpourri
Then it's time to actualize
And turn it into reality

Make the best use of your reverie
And design a gift that keeps on giving
Postmark it for future delivery
Then return to the present to begin receiving

We are capable of so much more than we recognize.

Transcendence

3 All that has happened
Is yet to occur
Especially such that do impend
Simply preparing to recur

2 Or simply lack the ability
To uncover what we suppress
And set ourselves free
To explore abilities we possess

1 To know without knowing
Access streams of consciousness
Yet fail to see what they are showing
Perhaps we regress

6 Beyond anticipating events
To actually influencing and more
Harness universal currents
Spread wings and finally soar

5 Imagine the possibilities then
Of recognizing and accepting
And acting based on an omen
With all the benefits of preplanning

4 Feelings, thoughts, perhaps events
Oftentimes do they portend
To comprehend universal intents
Just means not if but when

We sometimes encounter wonderful things we were not looking for and then determine that they are even more beneficial to us than what we had actually been seeking.

But if we hadn't been searching in the first place we might never have been presented with such pleasant surprises.

Serendipity happens when we create the right conditions.

Serendipity

Creating something is really as simple as
Believing in the innate ability one has
And accepting the premise that it will materialize
If one simply tries

It matters not how large or small the project is
Nor if one has the knowledge, skills, or abilities
The only difference that can portend
Is how long it takes to achieve the end

Any lacking knowledge, skill, or ability
Can be acquired in advance of the activity
Or in parallel with project execution
On the basis of continuing education

So long as a person has a vision
A burning desire to embark on a mission
The drive and determination to sustain the effort
And the sense of immediacy to actually set forth

On the mission that has been devised
The vision is bound to be realized
And required resources will be presented
At appropriate and serendipitous, yet intended

Moments in the creative adventure
As universal law steps in to support the venture
By rewarding ingenuity
And making things as they were meant to be

Committing to a prescribed course of action is your part of the bargain. The universe does the rest.

The image used on this page is intended purely as a metaphor and should not in any way, shape or form be construed as financial advice, or advice to sell your property.

Commitment

Fame or fortune, wealth or lack of it
Neither has bearing on the failure or success
Of anyone wishing to change a single habit
Or make a difference in lives countless

The creation of anything, material or not
Requires dedication and singularity of purpose
Such that one willingly sacrifices house and lot
And with laser like focus

Determinedly and continuously directs
All energy and attention
At the effort one expects
To bring the vision to fruition

And if the drive and dedication are of sufficient
Magnitude to compel such extraordinary
And unwavering commitment
One invariably encounters necessary

And unparalleled collaboration from the universe
In the location and acquisition
Of each and every resource
Required to accomplish the mission

The verbiage used on this page is purely metaphorical in nature and should not in any way, shape or form be construed as financial advice, or advice to dispose of your property.

Fame, wealth and power are only by-products of success. The actual success one achieves is the continuous development, refinement and repetition of habits and groups of habits designed to bring about a specific result or set of results.

Financial abundance is usually
the last thing to be realized.

Ultimate Success

The process of success is like growing a tree
All the way from seed to maturity
First there's the idea of what you want it to be
Then the effort to make it reality

The image you have is very clear
It's exactly the tree you intend to grow
You kick the effort into high gear
Selecting the right seed, proceeding to sow

Your faith in the process now really important
Initial efforts seemingly fail to bear fruit
While beneath the surface seed becomes plant
Builds a foundation and puts down root

And with absolute conviction
You continue your effort
Not entirely unlike the addiction
Of betting on a sport

Then one day a glimmer of hope
As welcome a sight as any you've seen
A firm patch on a slippery slope
Glistening in the sun a sliver of green

Newly encouraged you stiffen your resolve
In your eyes a sudden gleam
Lingering doubts quickly dissolve
You're on the way to realizing your dream

Beware, however, of the great temptation
To wait 'til the end to finally exult
The full grown tree is merely the culmination
Of multiple successes, just the end result

Each day you persist is a successful day
Every effort made a useful one
Despite the absence of an outcome on display
Celebrate the day when it is done

For those little efforts consistently repeated
Are the basic steps in a process
Which when diligently and patiently executed
Soon translate into ultimate success

The fringe benefit of the determined and consistent application of the creative effort is financial reward, a much improved lifestyle and lasting peace.

The IEAR Formula

Intentions + **Expectations** + **Actions** = **Results**

With the sun rising and so much to learn
You're ill prepared your stripes to earn
But the lessons get taught irrespective of thee
That is what you have come to see

Before long it becomes high noon
And you begin to think that one day soon
After doing all that there is to do
You will try to learn from the universe too

So late in the afternoon you finally focus
And as shadows lengthen all around us
When you should be teaching others the score
You're just learning what was taught before

But the mighty universe will always be near
Ready to teach when we're ready to hear
All the lessons we want and more
As long as we keep open the door

So you listen and learn and you're even more curious
And the lessons keep coming fast and furious
And then, one day you're forced to admit
It's not how much you know but what you do with it

Action

Unlike King Midas, your golden touch
will be a blessing, not a curse.

The Touch

Persistent yearnings for elusive dreams
Questing born of deep conviction
Conflicted passions, silent screams
Patterns characteristic of deep addiction

Physical journeys to places beckoning
Solitary roads you internally travel
Imaginary beacons all silently welcoming
Ensuring it doesn't unravel

Fraught with danger this frontier trail
Specifically, doubt and fear
Naturally designed to try to make you fail
They're like whispers in your ear

You tell yourself you'll succeed or die trying
You love what you're doing so much
You're not afraid of dying
Then you discover you have the Midas touch

Make the commitment and begin.
You'll soon be wondering why you waited so long.

The Habit of Success

Success is a way of life that must be totally embraced. It is a habit that must be developed and lived. Success is a personal growth journey.

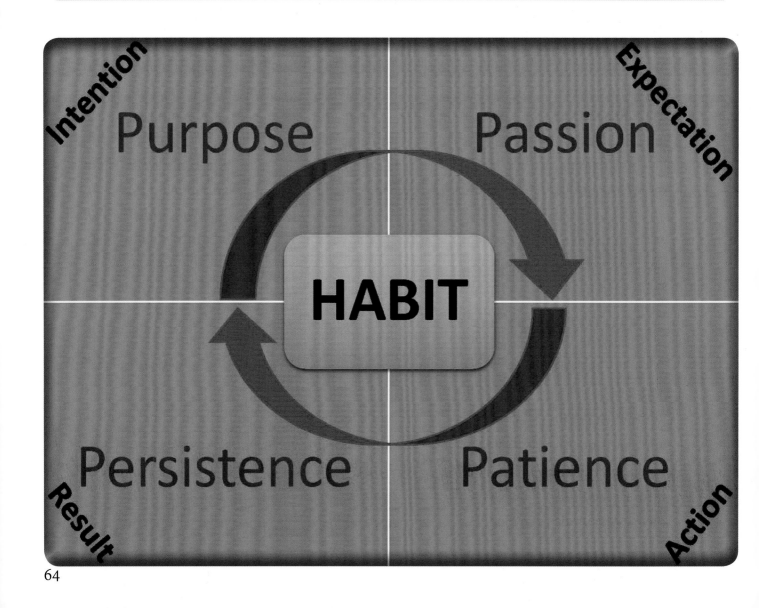

Overnight Success

Not dreaming the biggest dreams,
But you visualize your dreams more intensely than the scariest of
silent screams

Not the best planner,
But you know what you want, you want it more than anything else, and you approach it in
a serious manner

Not starting out with adequate resources,
But you utilize those you have to the best of your ability and somehow find
additional sources

Not the most knowledgeable,
But you research far and wide in the process of securing the necessary information, and
you become fully capable

Not necessarily the most talented,
But you've never worked harder for anything
you ever wanted

Not even the right habits did you possess,
But you had a burning desire and never stopped trying, diligently toiling in obscurity, and
suddenly one day ... you're an overnight success

*Success is not some status we suddenly
one day finally achieve.*

Visualization

Wispy, wandering winds casually caressing
Warm, welcoming rays pleasantly penetrating
White, watery sand the toes tenderly titillating
Winsome, washing waves the spirit serenading

Reverie interrupted
Attention co-opted
Totally unexpected
Nonetheless heeded

Searching eyes through contact lenses
Resisting mind puts up fences
Still relaxed, yet everything tenses
Focusing with all the senses

Each cresting wave more clearly revealing
Listlessly, dark object bobbing
Alternately showing then concealing
No, not a body, simply a log floating

Motionless solitude, curious gaze riveting
From what latitude secretly wondering
Feeling a yearning, wishing it were me
Aimlessly, casting about in the sea

Whoosh! Bang! Flash! Bright white!
Momentarily stunned, trying to get hold
Nothing in sight, just vanishing light
Suddenly wet, also cold

A struggle for breath
Not ready to go yet
Presently, I see
That log is now me

Loggie Log my name
Just Loggie will do
If that is too tame
Then it's LL to you

Sense of urgency as I near the shore
Ill prepared for what life would teach
Thoughts of a new life coming to fore
Excited, weary I arrive at the beach

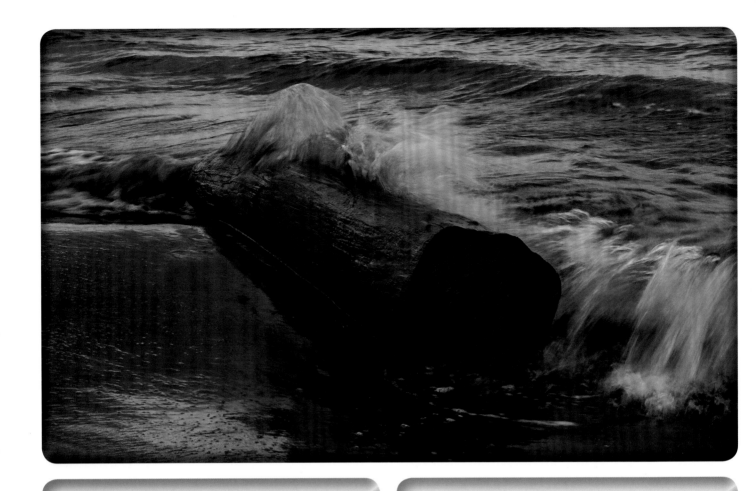

With loss of limb no longer a tree
Devoid of bark that protected me
A simple log all I have come to be
Silky and smooth for all to see

Considering the fate many logs endure
Insufficient reason to feel insecure
All I must do is make it onshore
Then aimless drifter nevermore

No nails, no screws, no drills, no frills
Neither barbed wire nor window sills
Better yet, not buried in landfills
Or even worse, filleted in sawmills

Truly blessed this Log has been
Living a life only dreamt of by men
Having grasped all there was to be seen
Time to come home to the land again

I gather myself for the run up the beach
Beginning to roll as I sense the next wave
It loses steam before I reach
I try again; I must be brave

Imagine children frolicking away
So too, I dance with the surf
This riveting drama no leisurely play
Just a desperate struggle for turf

Repeatedly denied, this mountain so tall
Too far I've come to give up now
Had I but one solitary limb, no trouble at all
Just a bit more time, I'll figure out how

Along the beach I drift with the tide
North to South, side to side
Gentler slopes and still denied
Definitely not enjoying this ride

Getting desperate to break through the fog
Wondering whether it could be my fate
To simply be just a waterlogged log
All bloated and very overweight

Right on cue I hear the voices
I will! No you won't! I can! No, you can't!
As they always do, arguing about choices
Enough already; stop that foolish rant

Dissenting voices, perish the thought!
They only win battles never fought
Many mentors I call to mind
All reassure, a way I will find

But scars of abuse deeply embedded
Flashing memories of scenes I dreaded
Unable to be totally avoided
Into my mind all now flooded

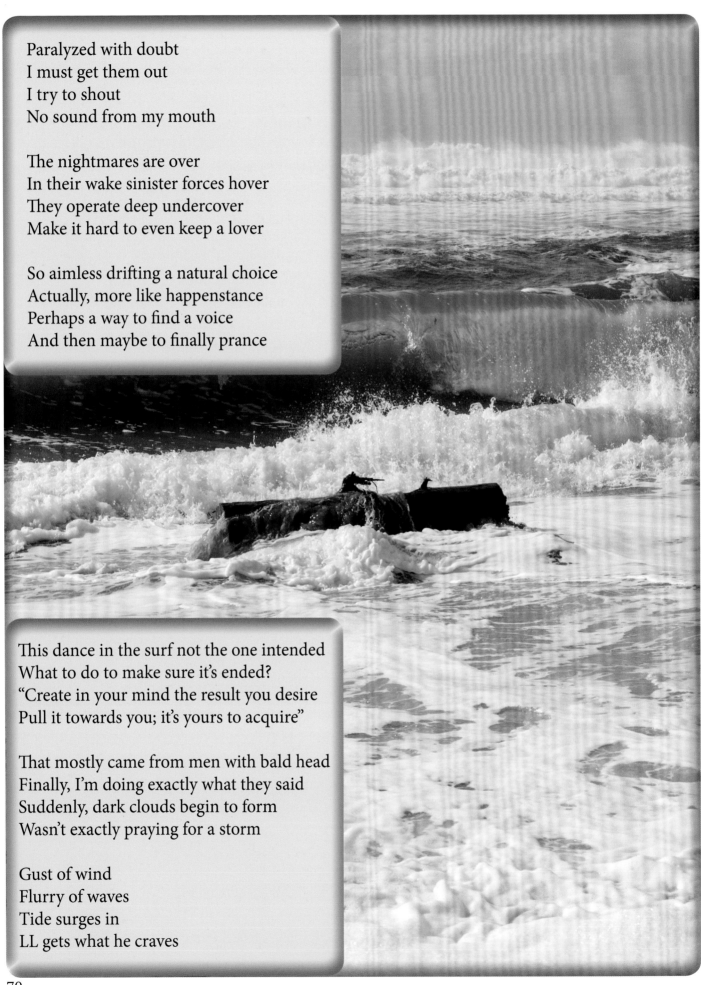

Paralyzed with doubt
I must get them out
I try to shout
No sound from my mouth

The nightmares are over
In their wake sinister forces hover
They operate deep undercover
Make it hard to even keep a lover

So aimless drifting a natural choice
Actually, more like happenstance
Perhaps a way to find a voice
And then maybe to finally prance

This dance in the surf not the one intended
What to do to make sure it's ended?
"Create in your mind the result you desire
Pull it towards you; it's yours to acquire"

That mostly came from men with bald head
Finally, I'm doing exactly what they said
Suddenly, dark clouds begin to form
Wasn't exactly praying for a storm

Gust of wind
Flurry of waves
Tide surges in
LL gets what he craves

Safe and secure I rest on the beach
Here I sit for all to see
All my dreams finally within reach
Exactly where I wanted to be

Almost as quickly the storm begins fading
Turbulent waters gradually receding
Not the work of a conjurer in the making
Simply the power of visualizing

All around me logs abound
Patiently waiting to be found
Very different from the crowd
I am distinctive and I am proud

A hearty welcome from a barking dog
LL's in luck; he's headed for the log
Sniffs around as a sign of respect
Cocks his leg for full effect

Big, black and shiny, wet as can be
Never nailed; not even screwed
Salty too from all that sea
Faith in the universe freshly renewed

LL lies there still as a log
Blank canvas for Salvador Dali
Getting blessed by this huge male dog
Unceremoniously marked as new territory

Sheepishly I look around
No one makes a sound
I must be in good company
I sincerely hope they like me

Many sizes, shapes and colors
Few like me and so many others
Some weather beaten
Others partially eaten

The closest ones begin to whisper
Perfect you are, but oh so wrong
You'll soon shrivel and crack like plaster
Without your skin you won't last long

Imperfect though most of us are
Sought by craftsmen from far and near
To be found soon and end up in a bar
The only hope for you we fear

About getting screwed, I'm very skittish
No free lunch, they all admonish
Even diamonds are subjected to polish
Those fears you must abolish

No pain no gain, always a price
Transformation is a laborious process
If you are willing to sacrifice
You will undoubtedly achieve success

Lessons now concluded
A good time to ponder
At least I know nothing's precluded
What's in store? I truly wonder

I visualize life as campfire seating
Perhaps right here on this very beach
But life under Uranus not very appealing
Better a table for serving some peach

Immediately, I resolve to change my destiny
I summon rain to wash off the wee
I will be discovered still dark and very shiny
In my mind I produce a mini movie

Raindrops falling
Dog barking
Mind searching; nature calling
In the surf I see Conan skylarking

Wow! That was one weird dream … Here boy. C'mon, time to go … Weird, really weird.

Hey Conan, c'mon let's go … I must! I must! Oui! Oui! ... What? Where are you going? ... Come back here!

Oh, all right let's have a look … Man, that's a nice log … I could make a center and two end tables … Sure would look great in the living room.

Why do I feel I've been here before? … "It's déjà vu all over again" … Why does that log look so familiar? ... Let's get the truck before someone else takes it.

Hey, stop that! … What do you think you're doing? ... Better not try that in the living room! ... You're gonna get us both put out the house!

C'mon boy! C'mon! ... Atta boy … There you go … Race you to the truck!

Hey! ... Wait up … That's not fair … I wasn't even ready.

73

Duality

And then you finally realize
In those wonderful moments when you fantasize
Are to be found
Wisdom so profound

And in the hallways of your mind
You no longer being cosmically blind
Thoughts, unharnessed from the tethers
Of all physicality literally hold get-togethers

Plotting strategy for materialization
At a lower level of vibration
And you partake of the sweet nectar, relishing
The labor of love and harvesting

The very building blocks upon which would rest, with exclusivity
The foundation for your future success and creativity
For it is in that inner sanctum that all things are first created
Then sent forth to be externally duplicated

All things and all futures already exist.

*Creating something is actually
a two-step process -
first acquisition and then duplication.*

BORN TO PROCREATE
BORN TO RECREATE

BORN TO CREATE

YOUR VERY OWN MASTERPIECE

BORN TO

BECOME YOUR MASTERPIECE

The master dreamed …
Vivid, colorful dreams of what his next masterpiece
could be

And as the master dreamed …
His subject as yet unaware that it was even possible
to dream

The master worked …
Day after day, skillfully crafting his work of art into
the masterpiece he knew it would eventually become

And as the master worked …
Even nights and weekends,
putting every ounce of energy into his new creation

The master played …
For it is more like play than work to
pursue the passion of creating one's masterpiece

Soon, the master became amazed …
As his masterpiece began to take on a life of its own
and help to fashion its ultimate reality

And as the masterpiece emerged …
It discovered that thoughts were transferred,
and it too began to sense the possibilities

Then, as the masterpiece went from seed to fruit …
No one could stop the combined forces of master and
masterpiece from visualizing and creating and literally willing the
masterpiece into what they both knew was its manifest destiny

And the masterpiece became complete …
As master and masterpiece each gave life to the other,
and that combined force was impossible to defeat

Masterpiece

Have you ever wondered if the day
When there was no more work, simply play
Would ever come along your way
Never worrying come what may?

Never thought you would see the day
When you would work most of the day
And at the end of the day be happy to say
That even work did seem like play?

What if eventually you saw that day?
Would you allow nothing to get in the way?
And simply play and play all day?
Olé? Ok, then let's play!

The Day

And don't get worried and run away
It really is ok to play
And work truly will always stay
Right there waiting 'til next day

So, come on down to the dock of the bay
You've needed to do this in a terrible way
Put your imagination to work I say!
Sorry, I forgot that's actually play

See that ship leaving the quay
Imagine yourself on it, all old and gray
But not so tired you cannot play
It's bright and sunny and it is Sunday

Nice, warm, beautiful day
And yes, Sun does deserve to have its day
So relax and enjoy this blessed day
And let your mind drift far away

For very soon it will be Monday
Who was Mon, by the way?
Did they actually mean Moonday?
The answer to that is probably yea

And why is there a Tuesday
Probably had a lisp and couldn't say Stu's day
But I do understand having Wednesday
Had to be marriage day, yes Weddins day

See how quickly time passes away
You're already at hump day
You get over the hump is what they say
When you reach the middle work day

Surely others must rue the day
Every week on Sunday
When its time to face another day
One of those that's called a weekday

But we're ahead of ourselves so right away
Let us get back to Thursday
Have heard of Thor and I have to say
Why would he have a day?

And they fry fish on what day?
The good day, that would be Friday
Then they rested the following day
So they're right? Rest day is really Saturday?

What then about when we pray?
Saturday or Sunday?
Don't get confused from being old and gray
We should pray every day

But the game's not over I dare say
So think way back to your heyday
Was that the day you made hay?
You weren't a farmer you baked clay?

You then arranged them in a huge array?
That was way back in the day?
Before you were old, not even grey?
Aha, you built the houses where we stay

All right, let's not go too far astray
In the distance that ship is fading away
Get rid of that toupee
You're back on the quay

There it is a very snowy day
And you're climbing up onto a sleigh
Nearing the end of a wonderful day
Getting whisked away to a grand soiree

Greeted at the door of this huge chalet
By a server with a silver tray
You suddenly wonder what to say
Then all your fears she does allay

Inside, the party very much underway
All manner of folk whiling the time away
Toasting to a happy, happy birthday
Bastardizing just about every cliché

And in another room just off the foyer
A more intellectual discussion on display
Easily finding words to convey
Cheerfully contemplating the origins of day

Wondering if night came before day
Or could it have been the other way
Either way happy they say
To celebrate another special day

Then they discuss Holy Day vs holiday
And how it is now just a commercial day
And all night they continue to yack away
'Til someone exclaims it's just before day

As husband ponders in an offhand way
Is day-light less of anything than midday?
Wife wonders cabernet or chardonnay
And how much longer should they stay

And as they stumble out to the driveway
Some holding on as they rock and sway
Very appreciative of the dawn of a new day
Wishing each other Happy New Year's Day

All too soon it's time to obey
The silent forces come to spirit you away
When you're tempted to overstay
With this wonderfully soothing getaway

Now suddenly staring at a digital display
On the dashboard of a red Chevrolet
Parked on a deserted, quaint, old quay
At the edge of the San Francisco Bay

Having just returned with a ray
Of hope, that is, from far away
Time for some café au lait
With a delicious serving of cheese soufflé

Okay, it's been a really incredible day
But that's enough for one day
So now, in the most heartfelt way,
It's time to say:

To some of you a Blessed Day

To others a Spiritual Day

The rest of you have a Wonderful Day

And to all of you a very, very Playful Day!

Afterword

Success

Among the greatest desires in the world one stands out as perhaps the most elusive – Success. Why do so many have such a difficult time achieving it? Is there a way of evening the odds? If so, can the average person acquire and learn to apply that knowledge?

We all have the ability to be far more successful. But the starting line is staggered. Each of us begins with a different handicap. Consequently, some must do a greater amount of preparatory work.

Success is personal. No one can define it for anyone else. We each have to decide what it means to us or we could end up chasing someone else's dream. And that would become the worst of all possible catastrophes.

One size does not fit all. We all come into this world with our unique set of challenges and lessons to learn and teach. And we continually add lessons as we progress along our journey to increased enlightenment, abundance, joy, and peace.

In his famous, bestselling book, *Think and Grow Rich*, Napoleon Hill said, "Whatever you can conceive and believe you will achieve". That very powerful and profound statement has been responsible for motivating huge numbers of people to pursue their dreams of achieving greater success.

But the statement, by its very nature,

suggests a focus on larger, more ambitious goals. And so, while it is an important first step in the process of getting to an ultimate end result, in the short term it must to some extent give way to a focus on the mechanics of periodic activities that are the essential building blocks of any future success.

In order to properly discuss success we must first have a clear understanding of what it is. The leading dictionaries are in general agreement on the two most prominent definitions:

1. The achievement of something intended, planned or attempted
2. Impressive achievement, especially the attainment of fame, wealth or power

Note that fame, wealth and power do not occupy the primary position. Neverthe-less, those are precisely the things foremost in the minds of people when they think about success.

It is not surprising then that success gets put on a pedestal and becomes this huge and almost unattainable goal, which lies only within the reach of a privileged few.

The irony is that the few who do achieve fame, wealth and power only do so because they understand these things to be secondary. Their focus is squarely on the primary definition. They clearly understand that this is the source of their fame, wealth and power.

That understanding goes well beyond the knowledge of what it can do for them. They have in-depth knowledge of how it works and what to do to make it consistently provide the results they desire. And they continuously do what it takes to make it work for them. That essentially is the secret of those most successful and powerful.

The good news is that this knowledge and information is available to all of us. Yes, you too can employ those very same principles and become a tremendous success.

Note, however, that fame, wealth and power are only byproducts of success. The actual success one achieves is the continuous development, refinement and repetition of habits and groups of habits designed to bring about a specific result or set of results.

Financial abundance is usually the last thing to be realized. Typically, a person experiencing financial success has already been successful on many levels. In a sense it is a reward received for becoming successful, and getting to that reward requires going through a well-established process.

Let's further deepen our understanding of success. I am convinced that success is a habit, and successful people have simply developed and exploited that habit. Why do I say that? A habit is really an action that is continually repeated until it becomes almost second nature. But a series of actions can also be grouped together to form a single habit. That is precisely the case with the habit of success.

And the most important habit one can develop and continually repeat is the habit of success. If in fact we are able to adopt this view of success and govern our lives accordingly, we will ensure success in every aspect of our lives on which we focus.

Now, while we may yet not be aware, the preoccupation with success is completely intertwined with the whole notion of learning, teaching, growth and evolution. For the drive to succeed is nothing more or less than the need to create, whether we are creating a better circumstance for ourselves, our family, our community, our country or the world at large.

We come from and remain an integral part of the ultimate creator – the Universe. We are driven by a deeply embedded need to create. It's in our DNA. We create careers, business entities, meals, schools, institutions, curricula, shrines, art, musical compositions, books, vehicles, fantasies, etc. We even procreate. Our greatest sense of fulfill-ment comes when we are creating something worthwhile.

Ultimately, that drive to create something better comes from the basic need of the universe to preserve itself, to preserve life, to adapt to changing conditions, to improve, to evolve. And it gives itself every opportunity to do this by virtue of plant, animal and especially human life. So, we ignore the deep-seated, creative drive within us to our detriment.

Conversely, understanding and embracing the relationship between our basic creative nature and the need to succeed is one of the critically important aspects of our existence. It is among the greatest lessons we can learn and teach. And it could become the most important factor in engendering the shift from mainly competitive to a more collaborative societal consciousness.

Success is not some status we suddenly one day finally achieve. The only way to achieve true success is to pursue the whole life approach. Success is a way of life that must be totally accepted, lived and experienced each and every day. It is a way of thinking, of feeling, of approaching life and of accepting and embracing one's own unique identity, complete with its challenges, rewards, sorrows and triumphs. It is a habit that must be developed. Success is a personal growth journey.

How badly do you want to succeed? If you were given a formula that guarantees success, what would you do with it? Would you file it away for future use?

Would you immediately begin to apply it with every ounce of energy you have? Would you keep it only to yourself, or would you make it available to others?

We should also strive to become successful at helping others. That means sharing our knowledge about the mechanics of success, as well as providing encouragement, mentoring, etc. One of the greatest sources of a sense of accomplishment and inner peace comes from helping others and collaborating to achieve synergy.

Steven Covey said it best in *The 7 Habits of Highly Effective People.* "Learning is never complete until you have taught what you have learned." He goes on to explain that if you approach learning with the intention of passing on the knowledge to someone else then you actually do a much better job of acquiring and internalizing the information. And when you hear yourself explaining the concepts to someone else they become much clearer to you.

That is a very astute observation. It also means that the student simultaneously teaches the teacher simply by virtue of being the student and allowing the teacher to teach. Such is the wonderful nature of caring and sharing.

Why are we here? What is our true purpose? We may yet find out while we still have a chance to do something about it. Until then, it is at least clear that two of our primary roles are student and teacher. We learn, we teach ourselves and others and we grow and evolve. Even at the cellular level we are continually learning. That is how evolution occurs.

In the final analysis, placing the right focus on the habit of success significantly enhances our ability to achieve goals and objectives and increases the potential for having meaningful success in all areas of our lives.

Yes, success is a habit – one of the best that we can develop. Let's do our utmost to develop it and assist / encourage others to do likewise. Repetitive duplication of the tiniest of successes leads to habitual replication of larger successes.

A great many people define success as attaining a high level of achievement in business or career, which allows one to take care of family, travel, enjoy quality leisure time and perhaps even have all material comforts. To them that may be the ultimate success. But exclusively focusing on this type of success can be detrimental to the chances of achieving or sustaining that which is sought. That level of success certainly does not happen overnight, unless one happens to win the lottery, etc.

The typical person achieving that type of success has had to experience multiple successes on many levels, which then add up to the big one. And those usually come after significant effort and sacrifice.

The very first level of achievement is the commitment to create. Many people desire something more but a great deal never make the commitment. An internal transformation takes place when a decision is made to create something.

When you commit in such a way you're actually committing to a life changing journey. The agreement made with oneself is the driving force behind consistent action. And each day of consistent actions is itself a success and should be celebrated as such.

The achievement of intermediate goals feeds the flames of creativity. Burning even more brilliantly they fuel the desire and will to continue the journey. Eventually, major milestones are achieved.

Before long, the ultimate dream becomes a reality. And you happily continue to pursue the activity. It is a labor of love. The achievement of pursuing your passion, being true to your purpose and creating the life of your dreams is the ultimate success.

Don't know where to start? No one ever knows how to do anything until they have done it the first time. So, you can either teach yourself how to do it, or you can have someone teach you. Either way you will learn by doing. Grasping a concept and executing that concept are two different things.

If you've gotten this far you undoubtedly have a strong desire to make the necessary changes. So, don't let this opportunity pass. Make a commitment to yourself and then begin your transformation journey.

When we are embarking on a new journey there is excitement and fear because we do not know what will happen next. That is okay. As each moment passes and nothing bad happens we begin to feel safer and more comfortable with whom we are becoming. Fear subsides but excitement remains.

Before long, we acquire the fringe benefits of the determined and consistent application of the creative effort – financial reward, a much improved lifestyle and lasting peace.

Yes, success can also be defined in terms of lasting internal peace. And internal peace, or the lack of it, is one of the most critical yet least recognized problems ailing the world. For some, there is no greater goal than to permanently replace lifelong pain and suffering with peace and serenity.

So, don't delay. Get started today on your journey of healing and transformation. It will help you to find and live your passion and your purpose, accelerate your personal, professional, financial and spiritual growth, become all that you were meant to be, and forever live in abundance, compassion, joy and peace.

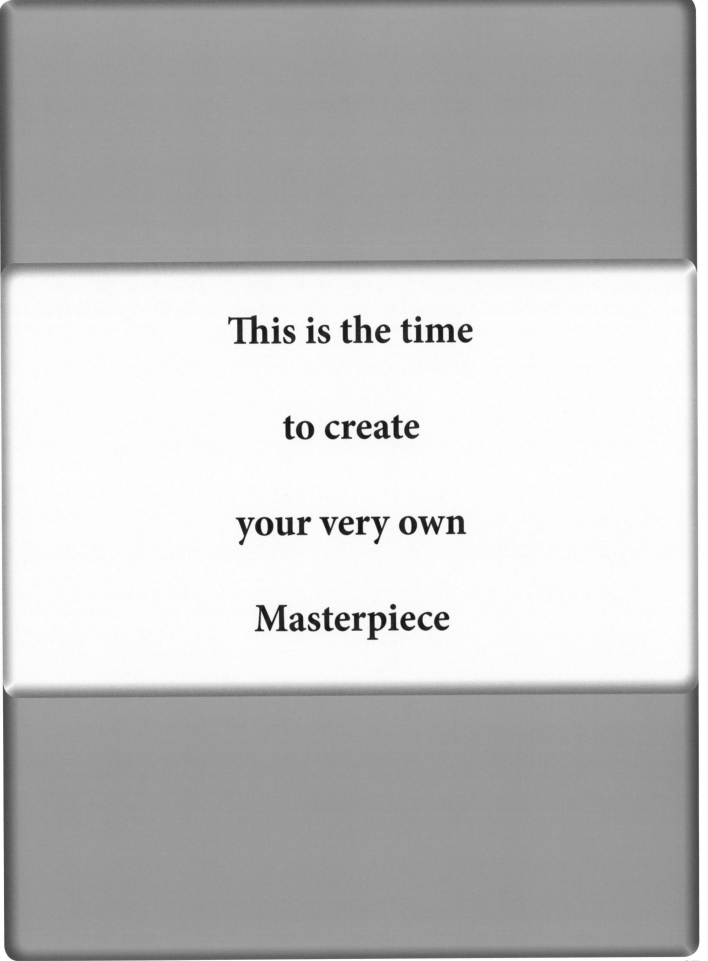

This is the time

to create

your very own

Masterpiece

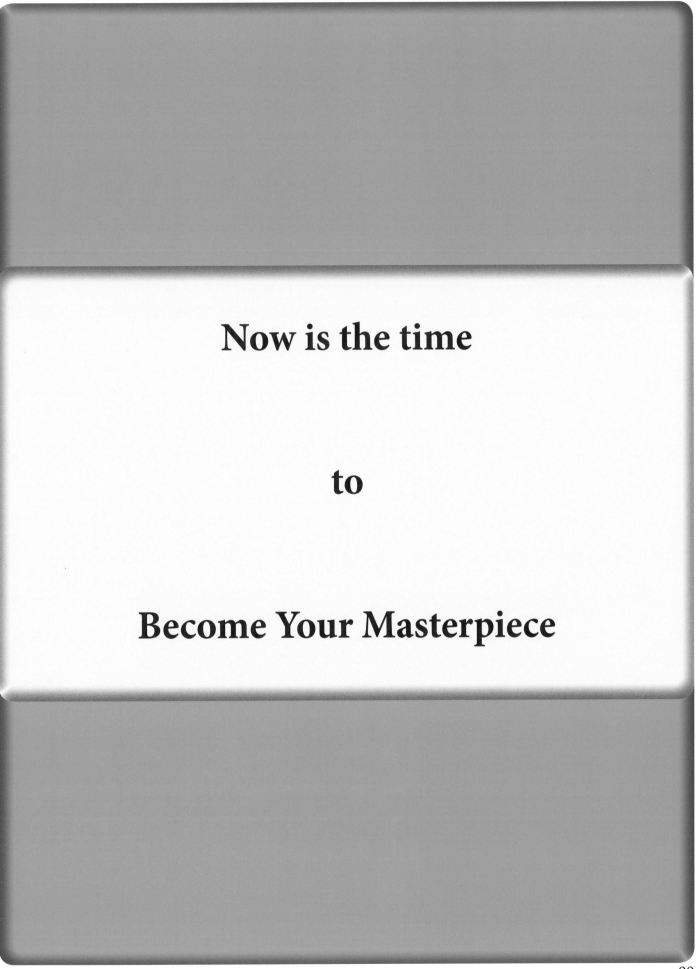

Now is the time

to

Become Your Masterpiece

The Beginning

Coming Soon

Become Your Masterpiece will also be available in paperback, eBook and audiobook formats.

The intent is to make this material affordable and available to all who need or want it.

BYM works for everyone but is especially effective for survivors.

Find out about upcoming books, courses and other resources at:

www.BecomeYourMasterpiece.com

Credits

The vast majority of the images used in this book were sourced from a few of the major stock photo vendors. A usage license was purchased for each image in that category. Consequently, no attribution is required for those.

Some sources provided images free of cost with the caveat that proper attribution would be given. A select few made them available without charge or requirement for attribution.

Nevertheless, artists should always be recognized for their creative efforts and the end product that results from those efforts.

The list beginning on the following page is an exhaustive one that gives proper credit to all artists in the latter two categories while only identifying the stock photo company from which each image was purchased for the former. Of course, sufficient unique identifiers are being provided so that one can easily track down the artist(s) through the company where his / her products are listed for sale.

The numerous graphics not credited in that list were created by the author. Many thanks to all those artists whose images are included in this book and helped to make it what it is.

Page	Name / Description	Contributor	Identifier	Location
vi	Butterflies	Adobe Stock	373776068	stock.adobe.com
xii	Temple Entrance	Shutterstock	332801474	shutterstock.com
xiv	Blue Lake/Trees/Snow	Photoholgic	UPY_iepQt5c	unsplash.com
1	Seagull in Sea	Dreamstime	1153609669	dreamstime.com
2	Lighthouse	Dreamstime	5809660	dreamstime.com
4	Full Moon	Dreamstime	35287489	dreamstime.com
6	Boy's Head / Dove	iStock	165636932	istockphoto.com
7	World	Bigstock	50255171	bigstockphoto.com
7	Jumping Boy	Mohamed Hassan	g7a51ec	pixabay.com
8	Shell in One Hand	Dreamstime	194560254	dreamstime.com
9	Man Reading Paper	Gograph	gg62502877	gograph.com
11	Shell in Two Hands	Dreamstime	12956272	dreamstime.com
14	Woman Brushing Teeth	Dreamstime	29650245	dreamstime.com
14	Man Shaving	Adobe	127842053	stock.adobe.com
14	Man Sitting on Toilet	Gograph	gg117892527	gograph.com
14	Man on Toilet w/ Laptop	Dreamstime	168601480	dreamstime.com
14	Showerhead Running	Shutterstock	1571565571	shutterstock.com
14	Bathtub	Macrovector	6203170	freepik.com
19	Bucket List	Dreamstime	33738929	dreamstime.com
20	Bicycle Rider	Gograph	gg66905053	gograph.com
20	Man Pondering	Shutterstock	1457039057	shutterstock.com
20	Baby Crawling	Adobe	222498857	stock.adobe.com
22	Man Sitting on Cliff	M. Venter	1659438	pexels.com
23	Green Valley	Tobias Bjorkli	1559821	pexels.com
24	Motorcyclist on Hill	Mathias Reding	12624894	pexels.com
25	Merry-Go-Round	Dreamstime	12255609	dreamstime.com
26	Divine Intervention	New Vision Art	14025_2	kershisnikprints.com[1]
29	Waterfall	Carmen Ong	1353242	pexels.com
32	Signpost	Adobe	137193688	stock.adobe.com
34	Man Under Tree	Dreamstime	257265990	dreamstime.com
36	Retro Wave Head	Dreamstime	88350581	dreamstime.com
38	Mule & Cart	Shutterstock	666874681	shutterstock.com
40	Blue Sky & Sea	Shutterstock	639799795	shutterstock.com
42	Meandering River	Shutterstock	2211968963	shutterstock.com

Page	Name / Description	Contributor	Identifier	Location
44	Synapse	Dreamstime	130096684	dreamstime.com
44	Lightbulb head	Dreamstime	172487711	dreamstime.com
44	Wi-Fi Head	Dreamstime	139654699	dreamstime.com
46	Man with Pole	Dreamstime	135020070	dreamstime.com
48	Woman with Eyes Closed	Shutterstock	1714244590	shutterstock.com
49	Eyes	Shutterstock	1175883970	shutterstock.com
51	Gift	Dreamstime	164673284	dreamstime.com
52	Woman with Gulls	Dreamstime	167829098	dreamstime.com
53	Seagull Soaring	Adobe	187482353	stock.adobe.com
56	House for Sale	Adobe	427680333	stock.adobe.com
58	Plant in Coins	Dreamstime	24609821	dreamstime.com
62	King Midas	Dreamstime	249182683	dreamstime.com
66	Woman at Water's Edge	Dreamstime	141558116	dreamstime.com
67	Log Floating	Dreamstime	60028952	dreamstime.com
68	Log Partially on Beach	Dreamstime	258043030	dreamstime.com
69	Log in Water near Beach	Dreamstime	258043034	dreamstime.com
70	Log in Green Surf	iStock	666849674	istockphoto.com
71	Wet Log on Beach	iStock	1339377154	istockphoto.com
72	Logs Piled on Beach	Dreamstime	4375678	dreamstime.com
72	Couple on Log / Campfire	Adobe	201875820	stock.adobe.com
73	Dog in Sea	Dreamstime	6119352	dreamstime.com
74	Tree Reflection in Water	Shutterstock	557494798	shutterstock.com
78	Cruise Ship	Dreamstime	150413983	dreamstime.com
80	Ship's Wake	Dreamstime	40504392	dreamstime.com
81	Horses / Sleigh	Adobe	407653391	stock.adobe.com
82	Chalet	iStock	155134782	istockphoto.com
83	Snowy Mountain Village	Maria Orlova	4969845	pexels.com
84	SF Bay / Quay	Adobe	181113041	stock.adobe.com
84	Red Camaro	Pure PNG	961524651721	purepng.com
85	Port of San Francisco	Adobe	3219191	stock.adobe.com
Jacket	Swallowtail Metamorphosis	Dreamstime	27046966	dreamstime.com
Jacket	Caterpillar	iStock	491904990	istockphoto.com

Notes:

[1]Divine Intervention, ©Brian T. Kershisnik, 2014. Used with permission